W9-CFG-663

Clever
COGZ

THE BOOK OF
SPACE ROCKETS

By Neil Clark

Quarto is the authority on a wide range of topics.

Quarto educates, entertains and enriches the lives of our readers—enthusiasts and lovers of hands-on living.

www.quartoknows.com

Author: Neil Clark
Illustrator: Neil Clark
Consultant: Oliver Green
Editor: Harriet Stone
Designer: Sarah Chapman-Suire

© 2019 Quarto Publishing plc

This edition first published in 2019
by QEB Publishing,
an imprint of The Quarto Group.
6 Orchard Road, Suite 100
Lake Forest, CA 92630
T: +1 949 380 7510
F: +1 949 380 7575
www.QuartoKnows.com

All rights reserved. No part of this publication
may be reproduced, stored in a retrieval
system, or transmitted in any form or by any
means, electronic, mechanical, photocopying,
recording, or otherwise, without the prior
permission of the publisher, nor be otherwise
circulated in any form of binding or cover
other than that in which it is published and
without a similar condition being imposed on
the subsequent purchaser.

A CIP record for this book is available from
the Library of Congress.

ISBN 978 1 78603 633 9

Manufactured in Shenzhen, China PP042019

9 8 7 6 5 4 3 2

MIX
Paper from
responsible sources
FSC® C001701
FSC
www.fsc.org

Hello, I'm Clever Cogz!

Follow me and my sidekicks, Nutty and Bolt, to learn all about rockets, spacecraft, satellites, and more.

CONTENTS

Space Rockets	4	Lunar Module	14
Rocket Design	6	Satellites	16
Rocket Flight	8	Mars Rover	18
Rocket Fuel	10	Space Station	20
Spacecraft	12	Space Shuttle	22
		Quiz	24

Space Rockets

Space rockets are giant vehicles used to launch things far into space. Cogz thinks that rockets are out of this world! Rockets help us find out about our universe.

Rockets are made from lots of clever parts. Find out more on page 6!

SATURN V rocket
This took astronauts to the Moon.

Types of Space Rocket

We have been sending rockets into space for more than 60 years. Some rockets carry satellites or robots, others carry astronauts inside spacecraft.

VEGA rocket

This one looks small, but it's still gigantic!

Which rocket do you like the best?

SOYUZ FG rocket
This has taken people to the International Space Station.

ARIANE 5 rocket

It takes a lot of time and money to make a rocket. Most of them can only be used once.

Rocket Design

A rocket is big at the bottom and has a pointy top, a bit like a paper airplane. This shape means it can fly through the air very fast. This is called being aerodynamic.

Saturn V
Cogz's favorite rocket is Saturn V. It carried a spacecraft that took three astronauts to the Moon for the very first time, in 1969.

Maybe you could be an astronaut one day.

nozzles

engine

Fins keep the rocket steady during blast off.

What the rocket is carrying is called the **payload**. This could be a satellite, equipment, or a **spacecraft** like this one.

fuel tanks

An astronaut is someone who is trained to travel into space.

Space Suits

It is very cold or very hot in space and there's no air to breathe. Astronauts must wear special suits that protect them and give them oxygen to breathe.

Rocket Flight

The shape of a rocket helps it to fly very fast. Before it is sent into space, a team of engineers check every part, down to the smallest nuts and bolts.

Cogz has always wanted to know about the exciting steps between take-off and splashdown. Let's take a look!

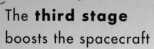

5
4
3
2
1

The **third stage** boosts the spacecraft toward its target.

The **second stage** pushes the rocket farther out of the Earth's atmosphere.

The **first stage** is the biggest part of the rocket. It powers the rocket during take-off.

BLAST OFF!!!

Rocket Stages

Most rockets are made of different sections, called stages. Each stage has its own fuel tank to blast the rocket further. One by one, the stages fall away once their fuel is used up, making the rocket smaller.

The **spacecraft** holds enough fuel to finish the mission and then come back to Earth. It uses parachutes to land safely in the sea.

woohoo!

Rocket Fuel

Rockets are very powerful! The first stage of a rocket needs lots of fuel to escape the pull of Earth's gravity.

The main fuel tank is the biggest part of a rocket. It weighs over four million pounds —that's as heavy as 19 blue whales!

Nutty and Bolt are taking a closer look...

Wow! This rocket engine is as powerful as 50 jumbo jets!

It's very loud!

fuel

oxygen

B

N

nozzles

How does rocket fuel work?

Inside a rocket, there's a tank of fuel and a tank of oxygen. They get mixed together and set alight, which creates a huge explosion of gas. This gas is pushed out of the nozzle very fast, which shoots the rocket upward. This upward force is called thrust.

Zoooooooom!!!

Have you ever blown up a balloon and then let go? The air inside the balloon rushes out of the nozzle, making the balloon fly around—a bit like a rocket!

Spacecraft

A spacecraft sits on top of a rocket and takes astronauts on their journey into space.

At the top of the Saturn V rocket was the Apollo 11 spacecraft. This is where the astronauts stayed on the first ever journey to the Moon. The spacecraft was made up of three modules.

oxygen tanks

nozzle

fuel tank

Mission Control
Astronauts in space can talk to people on Earth. The scientists that work in Mission Control talk to the astronauts using a radio.

Hello, this is Mission Control!

The engine was held in the **Service Module**.

hatch

The astronauts sat in the **Command Module** for most of their trip. It took three days to get to the Moon and three days to get back to Earth. **Can you spot who is inside?**

The **Lunar Module** was stored in a different part of the rocket. **Turn the page to find out more!**

thrusters

Radio Speech
People say "Roger" when they are talking on a radio. It means that they understand the message.

Roger!

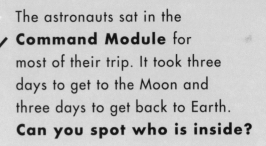

Lunar Module

The Lunar Module carried the astronauts from their spacecraft to the Moon's surface. Neil Armstrong and Buzz Aldrin were the first people to ever walk on the Moon.

When Neil Armstrong stepped onto the Moon he said these famous words:

One small step for a man, one giant leap for mankind!

Lunar Rover

Imagine driving on the Moon in this! This is a Lunar Rover, sometimes called a Moon Buggy. It couldn't go very fast, but it helped astronauts travel to different parts of the Moon.

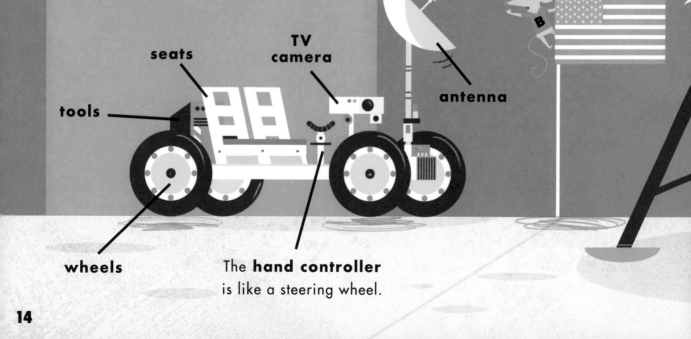

seats

TV camera

tools

antenna

wheels

The **hand controller** is like a steering wheel.

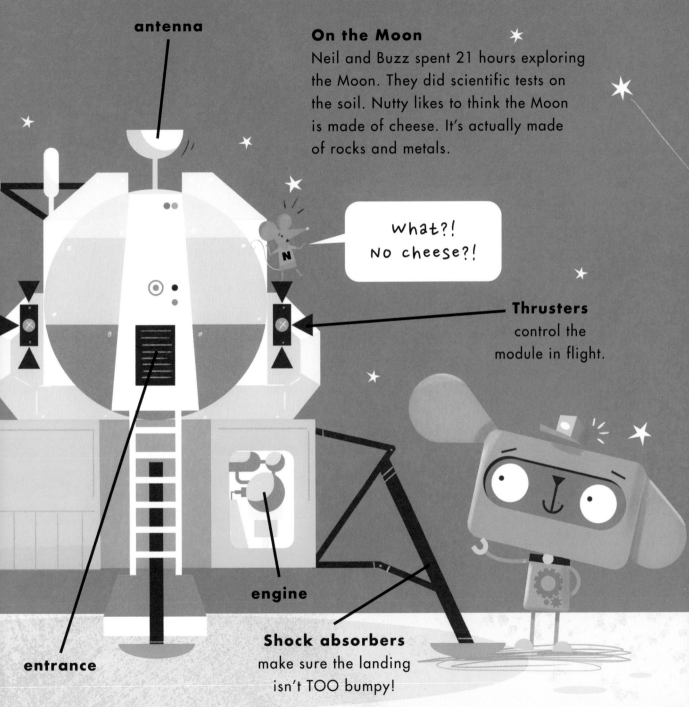

antenna

On the Moon
Neil and Buzz spent 21 hours exploring the Moon. They did scientific tests on the soil. Nutty likes to think the Moon is made of cheese. It's actually made of rocks and metals.

What?! No cheese?!

Thrusters
control the module in flight.

engine

entrance

Shock absorbers
make sure the landing isn't TOO bumpy!

Satellites

Satellites are objects that move around a planet or a star. They can be natural or human-made. Human-made satellites are blasted into space on top of a rocket. There are thousands of satellites circling the Earth right now.

> Hello, I'm Laika. I was the first dog in space! I traveled in a satellite called Sputnik 2.

What are satellites for?
Some satellites send and receive messages used for television, radio, and the Internet. This is the fastest way to send information across the globe. Other satellites explore faraway planets.

Sputnik 1
This was the first ever human-made satellite. It was blasted into space on top of a rocket in 1957.

Satellite Spotting
If you look at the sky when it's dark, you might see a satellite! They look like tiny dots of light moving across the sky.

This satellite is used to send and receive cellphone messages from across the globe.

Thrusters control the direction of the satellite.

Fuel tanks, batteries, and the computer are stored here.

The **antenna** sends and receives messages.

Solar panels take in sunlight and turn it into electricity.

The **Hubble Telescope** satellite sends us amazing photographs of places that are billions of light years away.

Mars Rover

Rockets are used to send robot explorers to other planets. Humans haven't been to Mars...yet! It's much safer to send robot explorers instead.

This robot is a Mars rover called Curiosity. It's about the size of a car and has been sent to do tests and look for signs of life. It has even found water on Mars!

Exploring Mars
Curiosity landed on Mars in 2012. It was launched there on a rocket called Atlas V. It used a parachute and rocket engines to land safely.

Say "cheese"!

CHEEESE!

Curiosity has 17 different cameras. It takes lots of pictures and then sends them back down to Earth.

This **laser** can turn rocks into powder! The powder is then tested to see what it is made of.

The **robotic arm** has a drill, a brush, and a camera.

I'm a robot explorer too!

These **wheels** have metal grips so the rover can drive easily across rocky ground.

The **nuclear battery** contains enough energy to power the rover for 14 years!

19

Space Station

Did you know there are people living in space right now? This is the International Space Station, or ISS. Astronauts live and work here for months at a time. Lots of experiments are going on inside.

The **docking port** is where visiting spacecraft attach. This allows people and supplies to get on and off.

Over 200 people have been to visit the ISS, including me!

The ISS is bigger than a jumbo jet! It has two bathrooms, a gym, and more room than a six-bedroom house.

Free Fall

The ISS is moving in free fall, which means that objects and people float around.

There are houses on Earth that have **solar panels** like these. **Have you seen any?**

Space Garden

Astronauts are learning to grow vegetables on the ISS. Onions, peas, radishes, and lettuces have all been grown in space.

Yum!

Space Shuttle

Imagine a spaceship that can blast into space like a rocket and then fly back to Earth like a plane. That's what a Space Shuttle does. Between 1981 and 2011, Space Shuttles were used to take astronauts on important missions.

The **rudder** helps to steer the shuttle during landing.

Having a robot arm is very handy!

wing

The **wheels** are used for landing.

tiles

Strong Skin

When a Space Shuttle re-enters the Earth's atmosphere, it gets very hot. It has a strong skin made from thousands of tiles to protect it. These special tiles are made from sand.

The **canadarm** is a robotic arm.

There have been five Space Shuttles. Unlike rockets, they can be used more than once.

The **star tracker system** works out exactly where the shuttle is in space by looking at the Sun and stars.

I love to look up at the stars, too!

These giant **bay doors** open and close to deliver equipment.

The astronauts sit in the **cabin**.

B

It's time to come back down to Earth! What have you learned about space rockets?

Nutty and Bolt have come up with 6 questions. If you can answer them, you might be as clever as me!

1. Where did the Saturn V rocket fly to?

2. What does "Roger" mean in radio talk?

3. Which planet is the Curiosity robot on?

4. Who said: "One small step for a man, one giant leap for mankind"?

5. Where are people learning to grow vegetables in space?

6. What was Sputnik 1?

Answers

1. The Moon, 2. The message has been understood, 3. Mars, 4. Neil Armstrong, 5. On the International Space Station (ISS), 6. A satellite